The Ultimate Guide To Inflating Your Trade Show Profits

How To Increase Branding, Recognition, Visibility, Customer Loyalty & Attract More Attention With BALLOONS!

Sandi Masori

Sandi Masori

Copyright © 2012 Sandi Masori

All rights reserved.

ISBN-13:

978-1477677261

ISBN-10:

1477677267

Table of Contents

ACKNOWLEDGMENTS viii

Disclaimer and The Legal Stuff. x

Why Balloons? 1

Exhibiting at Trade Shows 4

Having A Balloon Entertainer Attract Your Crowds 11

More Types of Decor and Their Uses 19

Business-To-Business Fairs. 28

Air-Filled vs. Helium 31

Digital Opt-In System. 35

10 Dos and Don'ts for Your Trade Show Booth 40

Biggest Marketing and Balloon Mistakes at Trade Shows . . . 41

Hiring a Balloon Artist. 43

California Balloon Laws – They Matter, Even
If You Aren't in California 46

The Environmental Impact of Balloons
- Are Balloons Green Enough?. 50

Balloons Outdoors 52

Are Balloons Elegant Enough For High-End Events? 57

Visibility/Attraction Opportunity for Service Companies . . . 59

Promoters Guide. 61

How To Tie a Balloon 70

Proper Balloon Sizing 72

How To Make a Balloon Water Weight 74

How To Make a Balloon Bouquet 80

How to Curl Ribbon 82

How To Get a Balloon Off Of The Ceiling 84

How Long Will a Balloon Float and Can You Make It
Float Longer?. 85

How to Make a Balloon Arch/ Column 87

How Are Balloons Affected By Temperature?. 91

Formula to Fill a Ceiling with Balloons 95

Testimonials. 97

Bonus Section : 102

Using Balloons For Grand Openings 102

Dear Reader,

First of all I want to both thank you and congratulate you for purchasing this book, The Ultimate Guide to Inflating Your Tradeshow Profits, How To Increase Branding, Recognition, Visibility, Customer Loyalty and Attract More Attention With Balloons! You've made a good choice.

This book is based on my heartfelt desire to help businesses get more out of their marketing. Balloons are often used for corporate events, but rarely to their full potential. With just a little bit of thought and strategy behind your balloon designs and multi channel media, you can dramatically increase your ROI (Return On Investment).

Who am I? I'm a certified balloon artist, a balloon industry veteran since 1994, a balloon industry educator, certified marketing technologist, platinum internet marketing coach, daughter of a pr guy/ journalist, and mom to two amazing boys.

Books in this series are built upon personal observations during years of events and tradeshows, as well as upon years of helping other businesses become more visible through online/offline marketing. Growing up with public relations and mega-events all around me started me upon this course.

You do not need to read these chapters in order. This is not a story. It's a collection of How-to's, Advice, Tips and Tricks to getting the most out of your balloons and your marketing. Read the chapter that you need for whatever stage you are in. I have tried to help you find the right balloon artist to work with, give you ideas of things to think about that will dramatically increase your ROI, and also provide you with some step-by-step guides should you want to do it yourself (I don't recommend it- better to work with a professional who can help you achieve all your goals, letting you focus on your business.) But for those who must due to budgetary constraints, or who are dyed-in-the-wool-do-it-yourselfers, there is something for you too.

Future volumes will cover nearly every aspect of utilizing balloons in corporate marketing. We'll look at psychology and the way to keep not only balloons but customers increase customer satisfaction and repeat business. We'll share industry secrets detailing how balloons can earn customer loyalty while building profits, and most importantly, we'll talk about the way to use your investment in balloon marketing to make more money and get more raving fans.

I welcome your feedback. Please feel free to email me at sandi@balloonmarketing101.com

Disclaimer and The Legal Stuff

The ideas, techniques and strategies presented in this book are just that. They are meant to inspire you and to get you thinking about your tradeshow booth with intent. I cannot guarantee or promise you what kind of results you will have- that largely depends on what you are putting into it, what your offer is, how you've positioned yourself, and message to market match.

I can only offer you the advice learned from years of experience and observations. The rest, ultimately, is up to you.

Why Balloons?

So, the first thing that you might be wondering is why would you want/ need to use balloons as part of your marketing plan at all?

Balloons can create ambiance, set a mood, create focal points, are highly visible and they make people happy. On a subconscious level, most people feel a little "warm and fuzzy" when they see balloons. There is something about them that brings all of us back to our childhood self. That's not to say that they're just for children, or children's events however.

The unique properties of balloons, and the way that they're a temporary art form, make them different than any other media. Balloons can float up high attracting attention from afar. They can be anchored to the ground, they can be framed, they can be in different textures and finishes, and the possibilities are only as limited as the artist you employ to execute them.

Balloons are highly visible and make people want to know what's going on. They are inviting and their rich color palette means that you can create any number of ambiances- from whimsical to elegant. By incorporating balloons imprinted with your logo, they are easy to use as a relatively inexpensive branding tool.

Balloons are appropriate for just about any type of corporate event, or use. For the purposes of this book we will focus on how to use them to get more out of your trade show booth, but keep your eye out for the upcoming books in this series: *Volume 2- Banquets, Meetings, Conferences and Stages* and *Volume 3- Employee Events.*

So since we're going to be discussing using balloons in your trade show marketing, let's start by giving you the first questions you should be asking yourself:

1. Is my booth indoors or outdoors?
2. What size/ style booth do I have?
3. Are there height or décor restrictions from the venue or show organizer? and
4. What is my trade show goal?

We will be discussing these questions and more throughout the book.

One of the things that I often hear people say is that they have had an expensive booth designed for them, so they don't really need to add anything else. That may be the case, however, often at the high-end shows, everyone has had a nice expensive booth designed for them, and until you are right on top of it, it's hard to distinguish one from the other. Even for these types of booths, balloons can make a huge difference, as you can see in the photos below.

Booth Before Adding Balloons

Booth After Adding Balloons

Exhibiting at Trade Shows

When you are exhibiting at a trade show, there are many things to take into account. The first is whether the show is a business-to-business show, or a business-to-consumer show. Each type of show may have different needs and a different approach to connecting with your target customer.

When you're planning your booth, it's important to decide what you are trying to do with it. Are you trying to attract attention from afar, sell products from the booth, collect leads, brand, or get your name out in the crowd? Are you trying to provide an interactive experience? Do you need to work around a height restriction (sometimes balloons are the only things that are allowed to be above a certain height...)? Would a photo-op area make sense for you? All of these goals are viable and can be realized or enhanced by using balloons.

Balloons Add Height and Enegy To This Booth. The Fast Zig-Zag Pattern Mimics the Feel of The Logo For This Energy Company.

Give some thought to the types and purpose of your decor. Your décor goals might be themed bringing in some sort of unifying motif- perhaps the company logo, mascot, or anniversary. Maybe you are going for a more whimsical theme, like tropical, or sports. It could be practical- simple décor in eye-catching colors to draw attention. It can be noticeable, high over your booth, to be seen from afar. It can be traffic-stopping- something so unique that people will not only stop in their tracks in front of your booth to look at it, but also tell others that they must go see it as well. It can simply be attractive, the purpose of which is to dress up an otherwise drab space.

Maybe you're going for ambiance: you just want people to feel a little bit happier when they see your booth. Do you have an island booth (center square full booth- open on all sides)? Then you have other areas that you need to decorate. You can create an inviting pavilion that people will be attracted to see what's going on.

This Topical Themed Setting Welcomed Visitor's to This Island Booth While Custom Artwork Let Visitors Know Whose Booth It Was

Colorful Balloon Columns and This Giant Balloon Greeter Stopped Everyone in Front of This Booth at The Electronics Show

There are some other concerns that you should take into account:

Non- Helium Venues

Sometimes venues say that they are no- balloon, or no-helium venues. Before giving up on the idea of balloons, check with your balloon artist to see if they are a preferred vendor. Many venues will allow balloons if they see the design first and know that you are working with a reputable balloon company, (and are not handing out helium balloons to people).

These Columns For a Wedding Show Incorporated Light and a Digital Opt In System to Capture Both the Brides' Attention and Their Information.

Hanging Decor With Magnets Works Well To Get Around No- Helium Rules

Logo Balloon

Cafe Japengo Had Their Logo Imprinted on This 3' Balloon For an Elegant and Custom Look

What size balloon you get depends on what you want to do with it. Balloons can be imprinted in 9", 11", 16" and 3'. I would stay away from the 9" if you want it to float.

Also, don't get the generic party balloons; what you save in cost you lose in poppage. Instead get a professional brand, like Qualatex. I would also caution you to stay away from doing the imprinting with the advertising companies- often the balloons they use are sub-standard, and the ink is borderline. Your local decorator can help you get professional quality imprinted balloons that will perfectly fit your needs and event.

Having A Balloon Entertainer Attract Your Crowds

Would your booth be best served by having an entertainer or balloon twister present? Having a balloon artist is a sure way to attract a captive audience to your booth. But there are three different styles of twisting for trade shows. All of them have their place, you just want to make sure that the artist that you hire is aware of your goals and purpose. Here is some information to make sure that you get the most from that investment.

Three Types of "Twisting"

- **Hired by Venue/ Organizer** -- Quantity is the name of the game here. Used as one of the event attractions and the objective is to distribute as many balloons to as many attendees as possible. Almost any balloon artist of a certain level can do this.

Expo Promo Style – In this style, the idea is to design quick hats and other visible items around a corporate logo balloon. Get as many people as possible to become walking billboards for sponsor. Speed is important here, but so is quality of design. In order to make the creations become "must haves" there must be a "cool" factor and something that goes beyond most people's perception of birthday balloons. This is especially important if making balloons for an all-adult audience. The balloon artist should also be giving shout-outs to sponsor whose name is on logo balloon. This style of twisting requires someone who is an advanced balloon artist with experience in corporate-balloon twisting. Designs can be learned for this style though, so an intermediate balloon artist would work.

- Audience Building -- This style requires advanced multi-balloon designs that take 10-20 minutes each. The sculptures, when completed must be a real prize and eye-catching. Balloonicatures, (which are caricatures made from balloons), and cartoon parodies work best. The point is to build a captive audience. The front of the line watches the balloon artist at work (who should include a pitch for the booth sponsor as part of his or her patter/ interaction). People at the front of the line have waited a long time to get their prize and their focus is on that. Those at the back of the line are standing in line because there is one. They're not committed yet (but they will be when someone walks past them w/ their personal balloonicature or caricature), but they are curious. The middle of the line is the salesperson/ spokesperson's dream. They are committed to getting their prize and have probably been there a bit. They are bored and ripe for a pitch. They'll listen to anything to make the time move faster. They will talk, opt-in, interact-- whatever the people working the line are looking for. It's very important to have a real professional for this style of balloon twisting. You need a master balloon artist who has experience with drawing in crowds, helping pitch them, and of course making the wow-factor balloon sculptures

These Fun Super-Heros Draw Crowds From The Entire Building

The Ultimate Guide to Inflating Your Trade Show Profits

Balloonicatures and Fun Themed Sculptures Will Engage and Entice Young and Old Alike.

More Types of Decor and Their Uses

Columns

Brightly colored columns can draw the eye wherever you want it to go. They're perfect to put large signs directing people to opt in to your list for a chance to win a prize!

These 2- Color Fast Pattern Columns Grab The Eye and Lead It to the Signs Directing Prospects to Text Into a Drawing.

Arches

There are many different arch styles. For the purposes of simplicity, we'll focus on the three main types here. What you really need to think about, as with all décor is: What purpose do you want the arch to serve?

SOP- string of pearls - more delicate, attracts attention but no visual clutter- can be high energy with fast color pattern and/ or ribbons or other things hanging down

This Booth Uses Fast Pattern String Of Pearl Arches to Stand Out From All The Other High End Booths.

Spiral- leads the eye up and down. Generally the industry uses the jargon "spiral" to mean any cluster packed garland, regardless of the design. Other patterns could be zig-zag, arrows, diamonds, flowers, etc... They are much thicker and heavier than SOP arches. They can be framed or helium. They are good for high ceilings, but look cluttered and out of scale w/ low ceilings.

This is a Perfect Example of a Spiral Arch in a Fast 5- Color Pattern

Herringbone - Middle between SOP and spiral arch. Flat on the bottom and has three straight lines. Can be used for a high-energy fast pattern, or a linear pattern.

Here is a Herringbone Arch in a Fast Rainbow Pattern

Balloon Wall

Walls, or murals, made out of balloons, are amazingly sturdy and versatile. They add an interesting texture that makes people want to get closer to check out. They can be used for branding, adding signs, logos and other effects. They are especially great for the back wall of a booth or a corporate-sponsored stage,or a branded, fun photo backdrop .

This Balloon Wall Makes Use of An Interesting Texture and Custom Logo Artwork

Balloon Greeter

Everyone wants to stand and take pictures with a larger-than-life balloon character greeter. This can range from full 3-D sculptures of your mascot, to column-based anthropods. It makes people curious as to what you're about and people will tell one another to go look at it.

It can also hold a sign directing people to opt in to win your drawing-- and they will! There's just something about getting directions from an 8' tall balloon effigy...

This Giant Runner Stopped Traffic, and Invited Questions and Photos from Trade Show Attendees

Cloud 9's

These whimsical pieces are excellent for outdoor shows because they are based on only one anchor point, and they don't have multiple ribbons to wrap around each other. They also have a fairly large presence and attract a lot of attention.

Cloud 9's Are Perfect For Outdoor Use! These Tall Cloud 9's Call a Lot of Attention To These Vendor Tables at a Golf Tournament

Bouquets

This is the generic term for a cluster of balloons that are tied on individual ribbons and then grouped together and attached to a weight. They can come in any number of shapes and arrangements.

These Bouquets Use a Tiered Formation and Stand About 9'- 10' High.

Sculptures

These are generally more custom and can either be twisted from the long skinny balloons (non-round in the industry jargon) or on a frame or skeleton- usually made from metal or aluminum.

This Giant Corporate Mascot Greeted Everyone At The Event and Invited People to Pose With Him for a Fun Photo Op.

The Ultimate Guide to Inflating Your Trade Show Profits

*Custom Sculptures Draw Big Reactions
6' Martini Glass and "RockWall Columns" Set An Inviting Mood and
Grab Attention*

Business- To- Business Fairs

At the smaller businesss to business fairs, like the BNI fairs or other networking group fairs, vendors often only get a table-top, not an actual booth

This is a good place for arches or other decor with a small footprint. Very few exhibitors will have anything nearly as eye catching

One small but eye-grabbing piece in the center of the table is very effective-- especially if that something carries a message, like directing people to opt into your list.   FORGET THE FISHBOWL! Instead, of having people drop cards into a bowl that you will never do anything with, refer to the chapter on digital opt-ins and utilize a system that will instantly and automatically follow up with people.

Table-Top Displays Can Still Be Fun and Inviting

Air-Filled vs. Helium

If you need your balloons to last for multiple days, it either must be framed and air filled or treated with Hi-float and helium-filled. Also, in order to keep it looking its best, and deliver maximum results for you, it should be maintained or refreshed daily. Ask your balloon artists about their maintenance services.

Right now there is a global helium shortage, so helium costs are going up and supply is becoming very limited. We are being very careful as to what jobs we agree to do far in advance because we don't know what the helium supply will be like in the near future. As of May 2012, helium cost to us has quadrupled, but at the moment we are still able to get it. In other parts of the country they are paying double or triple what we pay, and, in some places are unable to get it at all.

While helium balloons were once the easiest and most cost -effective type of décor, that may not be true any longer.

Everybody knows that helium is used for balloons, but because of its special properties, it's also used for the medical industry (MRIs), the defense industry, the welding industry and the tech industry (to make LCD screens). The balloon industry understandably takes last place in precedence of who gets helium. Right now the biggest consumers are the flat-screen manufacturers in Asia.

Why is it such an issue right now? That's a great question….

Helium is a non-renewable natural gas that is made from the decay of thorium and uranium. It is inert (doesn't burn), doesn't combine with any other elements, has a *very* low freezing point, and of course, is lighter than air.

There are only six companies in the world that refine and supply helium. There are only 15 sources of helium in the world, and 10 of those are in the United States. The helium that the US stockpiled is supposed to be liquidated by 2015, by order of the 1996 Helium privatization act. The federal helium reserve in Texas holds 35 percent of the world's helium. This federal facility has been operating at a deficit, and so needed to get rid of some of the gas. The problem is that they started selling it below market at a rate of 600 million cubic feet a day. Right now, the U.S. Senate is trying to pass a bill (The Helium Stewardship Act) to preserve the reserves. If it passes, the reserve could continue to produce helium until 2029. The prices will likely continue to soar though.

Besides the government "fire sale," there have also been shut-downs and extended closures for some of the plants, there have been issues with overseas facilities… basically it all leads to what some have called "the perfect storm."

Practically speaking it means a couple of things – anything using helium is going to get more and more expensive. What once was a great option for budget décor is going to become a very expensive way to decorate a venue. That is, assuming that the professional decorators still have supplies at all. In the meantime, we need to think of more creative ways to use framed and air-filled décor.

Don't fret though; there are a *ton* of gorgeous creative things that can be made from air-filled décor. In fact most professional decorators would probably say that helium only accounts for about 20 percent of their total business. So while we may lose the balloon on a string, the balloon professionals still have a lot of amazing options for you!

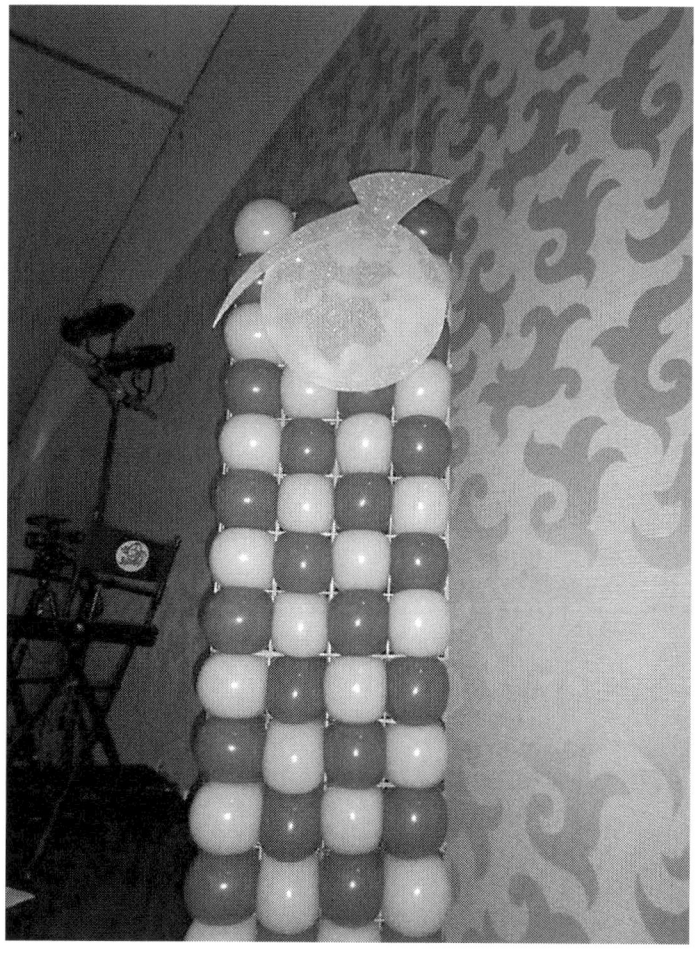

Digital Opt- In System

Now that you have a great looking booth that draws people in from all over, what are you going to do with those prospects? Are you going to hope that they come over and ask you questions? Are you going to offer a drawing or a contest to generate interest? Are you giving away Tchakes or swag?

Right now it's really popular to have a drawing for something in demand, like an iPad or a vacation. And while that's sure to get you a lot of names, what will you do with them?

Problem

A cool giveaway generates lots of written leads which then have to be manually entered into a database and tediously followed -up by sales people

Many of the leads are not even real leads- they're just people who want the give-away.

Wouldn't it be nice to have those leads automatically entered into a database, qualified and *automagically* followed-up by an introductory letter or other marketing piece? This leaves your sales people free to focus on only the hottest leads!

Solution

- Signs prominently displayed on colorful balloon columns attract attention from afar and direct prospects to text themselves into an automatic campaign.
- The system then initiates a text- message conversation which asks qualifying questions.
- The system also instantly sends out an email, so that your brand, message and contact information is in their inbox when they get home!
- ... And, because they want to win the prize, they open it.

A follow-up text goes out the next day asking for the best time for the sales rep to call to schedule a meeting

Those who answer that text are buyers.

Your sales people then know exactly who the hottest prospects are! And even better yet, the system also goes out and finds out how socially influential they are. (It does this by taking the email address and cross- referencing it with all of the social media sites to find out if they are active in social media) Not only do you know who your buyer is, you know who can best spread the word about you!

Benefits:

Visibility

"Cool" factor

Easy entry to database

Automagic follow- up and qualifying

Social influence score

Features:

- Large colorful attention getting decor

- Enter campaign via text, short code, qr code, Web, phone, email -unique individual local phone number

- Strategy coaching and campaign management by certified marketing technologist

- Cutting-edge technology that allows follow up by SMS(text message), email, webinar, voicemail

Try It:

Text name and email to 1 (858) 997-1604

Or text name email and keyword columns to 58885

Or scan qr code

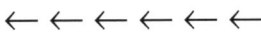

(If you go to my recommendation site,

http://www.sandirecommends.com , you will see a link to the lead generation system that I use and recommend.)

**** Important Note ****

If you are going to use digital opt-in (text, qr code, web-form, iPad), make sure that you have an extra person (or a few depending on show size), who is exclusively a "barker." This person should be VERY outgoing and stop people and get them to pull out their phones and opt in. This can be a student or contract person who doesn't know anything about your company- in fact it's better if he or she doesn't. You should be talking to people about your company and answering questions; they need only to get people to pull out their phones and opt-in. It's more important for them to be extreme extroverts than to be extremely beautiful.

10 Dos and Don'ts for Your Trade Show Booth

1. Don't block off a small booth with a table across the front (unless you have a really good reason), instead be open and inviting and get people to come in to your space and out of the aisle

2. Don't sit there and read a book or play on the computer. Instead engage your prospects, smile and call out to them.

3. If you have a really small booth, try marking the space out with painters tape and "rehearse" your set-up. Mark a 10x 10 space on the floor at your home or office, put tables in the space, and set out the items that you plan to display. This way you'll know how much you need to take with you and what can be left behind.

4. Find out what the venue restrictions are in terms of height and materials allowed.

5. Be clear on what your objectives are – why are you at the show? To get leads, to make sales, build brand recognition? All are valid, just be clear on what you want to get out of the show, or you won't know if it was a success or not.

6. Don't forget to do pre-show marketing. Let people know that you will be at the show, where to find you and why they'd want to.

7. Make a list and check it twice. Don't let yourself get stuck without something critical- write it all down and check it off

8. Never ignore your customers!

9. Have a show special, contest or a deal of some sort.

10. Don't forget to capture every lead and INSTANTLY follow up with them! The longer it takes to follow- up, the less likely that a prospect will turn into a customer.

Biggest Marketing and Balloon Mistakes at Trade Shows

1. Not paying attention to the purpose of the balloons – an arch may not be your best option- or it might be...
2. Not using balloons to help with branding and marketing
3. Not capturing the leads of every prospect
4. Not following- up with those leads
5. Not engaging with prospects
6. Not providing potential customers with a memorable experience
7. Not having a clear objective for your booth (branding, lead- capture, sales, loyalty- building, informational... etc.)
8. Not letting customers know your objective
9. Not telling your customers what you want them to do (ie Text your name and email to this number, Come to this area.

In this picture, the booth representative is doing a great job of engaging with her customers!

Hiring a Balloon Artist

Congratulations! You've decided to use balloons for your tradeshow booth or event! If you're looking for balloon attractions in San Diego, then of course Balloon Utopia is the answer :-). But, what if you don't live in an area that Balloon Utopia services? How do you know whom to hire? Below is a list of the things you should be looking for and the questions you should be asking.

1. Check their website. Of course, since you're reading this online, that's obvious. However, some balloon companies either buy pictures to put on their website, or "borrow" from other companies photos. Make sure that the pictures on their site are actually their own. Asking if they are using their own photos will give you insight into their abilities and ethics.

2. Don't just ask how much is an arch, it may very well be that an arch is not the best décor option for your event. Instead, work with your balloon professional as a designer, tell her or him what you are trying to do with the décor, and listen, or pay attention to what they recommend. This serves a dual purpose. You want to see that you are working with a decorator who understands the various design principals of décor. Additionally, the designer may know of some other options that are better for what you are trying to achieve. You really want to work with a designer, not just an order-taker.

3. When calling for quotes, make sure you're very specific. Though you may get a wide range of prices, you need to be certain that you're comparing apples to apples. Sometimes the cheapest is the best for your needs, and sometimes cheapest can be devastating.

4. One way to see what kind of company you are talking to is to ask for a price on something and see whether they just quote the price to you, or if they ask you more questions to get a better picture of what you really need. They should be asking you questions like what is the purpose of the décor, whether it's outdoors or indoors, what size you're talking about, etc...
5. Here are some questions that you might want to ask:
- Do they only do classic décor or do they do custom designs to fit your particular needs?
- Do they practice "deco-twisting" techniques (using balloons and techniques from the round and non-round sides of the balloon industry)?
- Will they help you with the design process by coming up with ideas?
- What is their experience? What type of events do they specialize in?
- Do they go to conventions to keep their skills fresh and to stay up on the latest techniques?
- Do they know the California balloon laws? Do they follow them? Even if you don't live in California, this is really important.
- Have they done events at that venue before? Are they familiar with the particular rules and regulations of that venue?
6. Tell them your budget and see what they recommend. They may very well give you ideas that you wouldn't have thought to ask about.

Here is a list of the type of issues you should discuss with your balloon artist:

1. Your vision- what kind of ambiance are you trying to create, what is the purpose of the decor?

2. Color Scheme or theme

3. Budget- Don't be afraid to talk about your budget in the first meeting. It will help your balloon artist steer you in the right direction and set priorities for the decor. After all, if you only want to spend $1000, there's no point in your decorator showing you tons of photos of $3000 sculptures. Similarly, if you are doing a high-end event, with a huge budget, you might want to know about the exploding balloons and the balloons with lights inside of them. Some clients worry that by telling the budget from the beginning, the prices will change accordingly. While designers may put together some custom packages to work with tight budgets, candor about budget lets them know which options to show you. If you are working with a reputable company, you shouldn't worry that they will behave unethically. The more information you give them, the better they can help you.

4. Timeline – When do things need to be set up and taken down, and how long do they need to last?

California Balloon Laws – They Matter, Even If You Aren't in California

Did you know that there are special balloon laws in California? Did you even know that there was such a thing as balloon laws?

Here in California we have balloon laws that the rest of the country doesn't have... yet. But even if you're not in California, it's important to know about the balloon laws.

Why you ask? Because mylar balloons that are let loose could cause power failures. That's what the laws are all about. Below is a quick summary of the California balloon law...

1. Every helium- filled foil balloon, (or electrically conductive material containing a gas lighter than air), must be anchored to something heavy enough to hold it down. It can be a fishing weight, a washer, a cute little plastic weight, etc., just so long as it's heavy enough to hold it down.

2. Don't tie metallic or electrically conductive ribbon to ANY helium balloon

3. Don't group foil balloons together in one bunch- individually tie each balloon to the weight.

4. Don't do balloon releases with foil balloons

There's a bit more, but that's really the gist of it. It's really important to follow them because loose foil balloons theoretically could put out the lights for a whole neighborhood. In California we almost even lost the right to sell helium-filled foil balloons. If we don't use them responsibly, we could lose the fun and excitement that foil balloons can bring to an event. And if it almost happened here, it could happen in other places too...

For more information on former Gov. Arnold Schwarzenegger saving the balloon, here's a reprint of an article I wrote on my blog a while back (http://www.balloonutopia.com/blog ...

Gov. Schwarzenegger saves the balloons!

In April 2008 Senate Bill 1499 was introduced in the State Senate Public Safety Committee. Introduced to the Senate by Senator Scott and the power companies, who contended that mylar balloons could cause massive power failures. The bill would have made it a crime for any person to sell or distribute any balloon that is constructed of electrically conductive material, and filled with a gas lighter than air, or any balloon filled with a gas lighter than air that is attached to an electrically conductive string, tether, streamer, or other electrically conductive appurtenance, except as specified. The lobbying efforts of the balloon industry succeeded in bringing about a compromise, although the bill's passage still would have meant significant changes in the use of mylar balloons here in California.

After passing the Senate and the Assembly, SB1499 was vetoed by Gov. Arnold Schwarzenegger who determined that other bills were a higher priority for the State of California. There is already a balloon law in place here in California. Current law mandates that helium-filled balloons be affixed to weights, attached to ribbon made of non-conductive material, and feature a label warning of the dangers of releasing balloons into the atmosphere. The current law has been in effect since 1990.

Although the balloon industry dodged this bullet, it's important for anyone who puts on events, or uses balloons, to be aware of the current balloon laws, and make sure that they are followed, so that we don't again face an all-out ban on helium-filled mylar balloons. In practical terms, what does this mean? It means that decorators in California can't make helium- filled arches out of mylar balloons, unless there is an anchor attached to each and every one of those mylar balloons-which would make it perfectly appropriate décor for the back of the stage, or as a wall dressing, but not for over a dance floor or an entry way. Also, mylar balloons cannot be used as free-floating balloons on the ceiling. In a room with panel ceilings, however, the same look could be achieved by hanging air-filled mylar balloons from the ceiling. One last tip: Often at events, guests would like to take some of the balloons home with them. Having some extra balloon weights on hand would enable your guests to take their souvenir home, without violating the California balloon laws, or running the risk of inadvertently causing a power failure.

This Star Cluster Column Uses Air-Filled Mylar Balloons For Big Impact

The Environmental Impact of Balloons - Are Balloons Green Enough?

Many people wonder about the environmental impact of balloons. Contrary to popular belief, balloons are one of the most environmentally friendly decor media around! Here are a couple of fun facts about balloons and greenness.

Balloons come from the sap of the rubber tree, *Heveabrasiliensis*, which grows in Malaysia. This sap looks like milk and is shipped to America in large ocean tankers. Once it is removed from the tree, the sap is called latex.

Balloons are biodegradable; they decompose at the rate of an oak leaf.

Balloons are environmentally friendly! Because they are made from the sap of a tree, in order to make more balloons, old trees must be preserved and more trees must be planted!!!!! In fact, each tree only produces enough latex for about 2 balloons a year- so every new 100 count bag of balloons means that 50 more trees that must be planted!

Something that is important to note however, though the latex balloons are completely green, mylar balloons are not. Mylar balloons do not biodegrade, although being made from metal and plastic, they are recyclable.

If you are planning to use balloons for balloon releases, make sure that you check with the FAA to ensure that you are not in a flight path so as not to cause an accident. Besides getting FAA permission, make sure that the balloons are attached to cotton string which will biodegrade, rather than a poly ribbon, which will not biodegrade.

If you are planning on doing balloons outside, make sure that you are following the California balloon laws, even if you are not in California. It's just responsible balloon use (see article in this book for more information on the California balloon laws.)

For indoor events, make sure that your guests know about responsible balloon use. Make it easy for them to be good citizens, if you are planning to send balloons home with the guests, make sure that the balloons are anchored to a weight so they won't accidentally be released.

With proper thought and care, balloons are one of the most environmentally friendly decor media out there!

Balloons Outdoors

Here in my hometown of San Diego, the mild climate invites people to host many events outdoor. That means picnics, barbecues, expos and public events. And of course, you want to decorate all your events with balloons.

Balloons are a great medium for attracting attention, adding color and ambiance, and setting the stage. The thing is, balloons outside have different needs and issues than balloons indoors.

First thing to watch out for is heat. Heat can wreak havoc on balloons in many ways. Stay away from dark colors, like black, green, brown, purple, etc., as they absorb heat and can pop. Next inflate the balloon so that it will float, but leave a little bit of room for the balloon to expand, so if the temperature warms up throughout the day, the balloon won't expand and pop.

Next thing you have to worry about is wind. As little as four miles an hour is a lot to a balloon. Essentially, the balloon is like a kite or a sail, it can catch the wind and be pushed by it. This means that for free-standing décor, like columns or arches, you want a solid base with a good footprint and weight. Weight alone is not enough, you also need a wide footprint.

Here are some recommendations for strategies to change indoor décor to something that would work better for outdoors:

Arches: Instead of a spiral arch, which is anchored to the ground, it's better to do two columns with wide footprints and have an arch tied into them. The arch can blow down to its anchor point. So, if it's anchored on the ground it can blow all the way down to the ground. If, on the other hand, it's anchored at the 6' mark of a column, it will generally only blow down to that point.

Bouquets: Instead of a bouquet with lots of individual ribbons, which will tangle around each other in the wind, it's better to do décor that is on a single anchor point, like a Cloud 9 or a Topiary kite. Then for extra movement you can put a wide ribbon hanging down to catch the wind and give some rhythm. The single anchor point will work better with the wind, moving from side to side instead of tangling up in itself.

Balloon Releases: Check your local city ordinances. Here in San Diego there are restrictions on how many balloons can be released, and releases are never allowed under the flight path or near beaches or bays. Balboa Park doesn't allow balloons of any kind. NEVER do a balloon release with foil balloons. See our section on the California balloon laws for more information on that.

Other types of décor that are very effective for outdoors are floating columns, streamers and hi-flyers.

Linear Columns and Floating Mini Columns Attracted Attention at This Outdoor Event

Giant Balloon Greeter Calls Everyone To Come Inside The Hospitality Tent

Are Balloons Elegant Enough For High-End Events?

Are balloons only for children's events? Can they be used for more elegant events? Yes! Balloons are an amazingly versatile medium that can be made to look as elegant or whimsical as the rest of the event. If you use bright colors and youthful themes, they're perfect for children's events. But what about for more upscale events? By using colors that have a high contrast- black and white, black and silver, black and gold- the effect can be very high-end and elegant.

Adding mylar balloons for the glitziness, or putting lights inside the balloons can further increase the breathtaking effect.

Talk to your balloon artist and see what ideas they have to bring elegance to your event.

Balloon "Awesome" Columns Incorporate Lights and a High-Contrast Color Scheme To Set The Mood.

High-Contrast Color Schemes and Lights Create Very Elegant Effects

Visibility/ Attraction Opportunity for Service Companies

Sponsor balloon decor/ entertainment for a non-profit event and get your brand and message everywhere when normally you'd be restricted to a plain table... Ideal for service industries that are traditionally less engaging (tax, insurance, finance, real estate, etc....) Build goodwill and get people excited

Non- profits are always asking balloon artists for both decor and entertainment at free or reduced costs. Many balloon artists say yes to as many events as they can, but donation requests far exceed their ability to do them all. Get together with a balloon artist in your area and have them notify you when they get such requests. If the group meets your target demographic- sponsor them! You'd be amazed at where those requests come from-- golf tournaments, church/ synagogue/ school functions, charities for medical causes, homeless-- you name it... some of them are sure to attract your exact audience!)

If you want to take that branding even further, and you're sponsoring a balloon artist to twist balloons at the non profit event, you could get a special Tshirt printed up that the balloon artist could wear that has your name and logo on it- or says "Balloon art courtesy of your company". Then, on the back you could have a big QR code that when scanned would take people either to your website, or better yet, to an opt in form to enter a drawing (and your data base). It's cheaper than you might think to make these. I often will print up my own t-shirt transfers, and then take them to one of the tourist t-shirt shops in town. They have a big heat press which will iron on the logo. If you make friends with them, they may even sell you the t-shirt for just above cost. Even if it's a bit more than that it's a very effective advertisement for you.

Promoters Guide

There are three stages of event marketing phases- Before (how to let people know about your event), during (what's happening at the event, what's the event experience), and after (how to keep people talking about it and connecting).

How can balloons help each stage?

Before- by helping to defray costs.

During- attraction and navigation.

After – lasting memory, branding and continuing to spread the message.

BEFORE

In the first stage, the question is how to fund the event, how are people (target audience/ public) going to learn about the event, how will they get there, and other logistics. Believe it or not, this is actually the best time to bring in your balloon artist. Media partners are often sought at this stage. Balloons can help you with this by being an attraction- like a world- record attempt, or a large sculpture.

Make large balloon sculptures a revenue source by selling sponsorship of pieces. Let's say that your event has a tropical theme, you could have various large tropical themed sculptures- a hula dancer, a palm tree, a tiki mask, a mermaid perhaps... Each of these pieces can be presold to exhibitors as part of a branding package. Say that the balloon artist charges

$500 for the piece, you can charge $1000 for the sponsorship opportunity. The piece will display the sponsor's name and booth number. Make it even more valuable and add dimension by offering the integration of mobile marketing packages and other lead- generation systems. (If you go to my recommendation site, Http://www.sandirecommends.com , you will see a link to the lead generation system that I use and recommend.)

Balloons can also be a giveaway- drawing people to that space or area—again in our tropical theme, maybe each balloon twister will only be twisting a single design, and participants must move through the event to see/ receive multiple designs. Sell sponsorships for placement and to draw the crowd to a given area. Balloons are a valuable giveaway- the balloons that make it home last for a very long time. By bringing your balloon artist in early, you can increase your exhibitor funding and sponsorship opportunities.

The Ultimate Guide to Inflating Your Trade Show Profits

Sandi Masori

DURING

What's going to happen during the event? When you walk through the event how do people arrive, how are they met, do they need tickets, what is the registration process, what do you want them to see, how will they get to places within the venue, how will they know where each area is, will there be a program, who will hand them out?.... So many intricate details. Balloons can be used to help the crowd navigate through the event. By using balloons in the same colors/ theme they can mark important focal points, directions, or areas. They can also create an environment for the stage area that is highly brandable and photographed.

Photo- op areas will also help the crowd navigate and provide a souvenir opportunity.

Balloon entertainers are great for crowd control. They capture peoples' attention, entertain them when there are long- wait lines, and add an element of fun that might otherwise not be there.

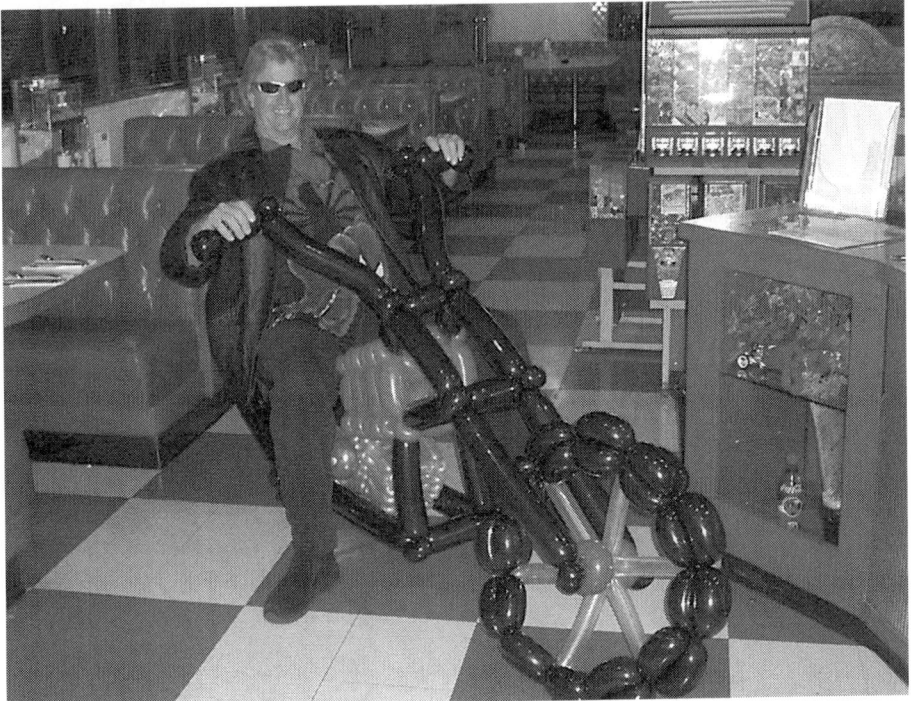

Master Balloon Artist Ken Stillman takes a "ride" on this photo-op bike

AFTER

Think Disneyland- souvenir photos can be put up on social media, on a Facebook page behind a likegate, on Flickr, on your event website. These photos should be branded with the show info. Cute photos of people with their balloons will be not only downloaded, but shared. Balloons make people happy. Create a viral after campaign.

In short, balloons can help you navigate people through the exhibit spaces, can help defray costs of putting on event, and can create an electronic memory that will build audience for you and your sponsors!

In summary, to get the maximum value out of the balloon décor, understand their role in ambiance, traffic control, harmonizing the theme or purpose of the event, and adding interactive fun.

How To Tie a Balloon

First of all, it's a lot easier to follow the instructions in a video format rather than in a written format. For best results visit my YouTube channel under the channel name Sandiballoon (http://www.youtube.com/sandiballoon).

Now, having issued that disclaimer, here are the instructions:

1. For a 260 balloon (the long skinny modeling balloons), before tying it, give it a good burp to release some of the pressure. Don't release so much air that you change the size of the balloon, but just enough to release some of the pressure and make it more manageable. If you can't stretch the nozzle around your fingers, let a little more air out. (This is not the case for round balloons)

2. Lay the balloon across your palm and thread the nozzle through your middle and ring fingers.

3. Wrap the balloon around the back of your middle finger and pointer finger.

4. Bring the nozzle around your fingers until it crisscrosses with the inflated portion of the balloon.

5. Open your middle finger and pointer fingers, so that you create a hole that you can tuck the nozzle through.

6. Put the nozzle up through the hole, hold onto it with the thumb and pointer finger of the hand that is not wrapped in the balloon and remove your fingers from being wrapped in the balloon (while holding the nozzle with

your other hand so it doesn't come back out with your fingers). This is the method that works best for me. Other people have other methods, so you really have to find the method that works the best for you. Some people prefer to wrap it around their thumb and pointer finger- but most balloon artists will agree that it's far easier to tie if you wrap it around two fingers rather than just one.

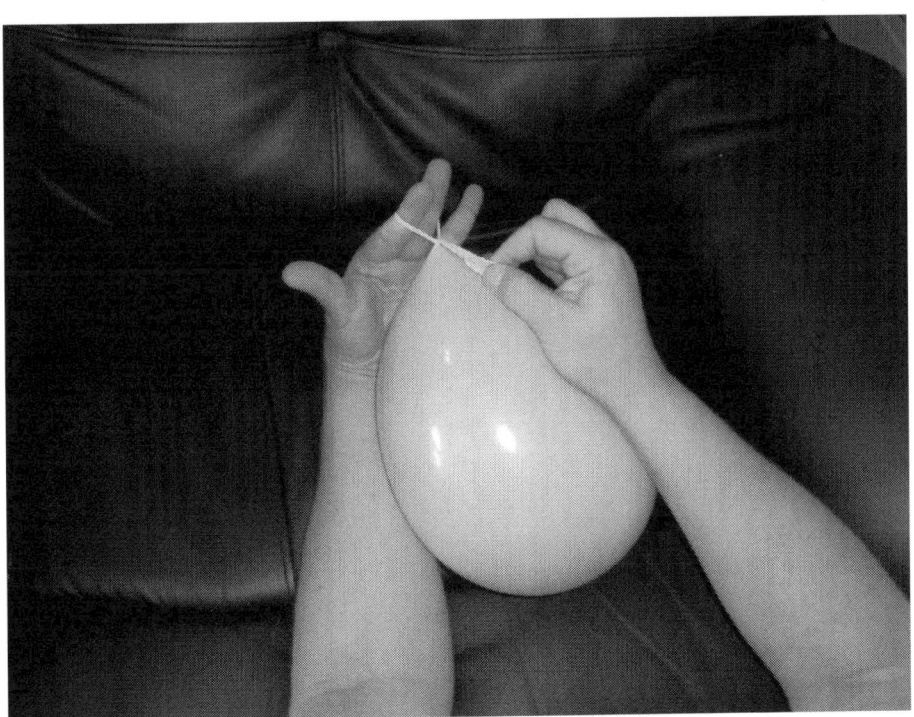

Proper Balloon Sizing

Sizing a balloon should be a simple thing, right? You just blow and blow until it's full, don't you? Not exactly.... in this article, I'll explain to you exactly how to get the right size for your balloon.

First of all, not all balloons are created equal. Some have the traditional balloon shape, and some have more of a round shape. For this article, we'll assume the balloons you are using have a traditional shape. The brands of balloons that I like best are Qualatex and Betallic.

The general rule of thumb is that a balloon shaped like a tear drop is properly inflated. If the balloon looks like a light bulb, on the other hand, then it's too full and will probably pop. If it looks like a ball, it's not full enough, and may not float (if filled with helium).

Sometimes you may want to under-inflate your balloons. If you're building some air-filled decor and it's going to be outside on a hot day, you may want to make those balloons nice and round so that they are fairly squishy and have room to expand.

If you are filling the balloons with helium, you usually will want to fill them to the proper size so that they will float and last the right amount of time.

When would you want to over-inflate the balloons? Well, I guess if you were doing something where having fragile balloons would be an advantage- if you are using water balloons for example, or if you are playing a balloon popping game.

How can you make sure that you size your balloons consistently? Take a box and cut squares out in the sizes you want, ie 4", 7", 9", 11" etc. Then inflate the balloon larger than what you think the right size might be. Slowly let the air out until it just clears the hole in the box. Bring it back up and tie it. Repeat on the next balloon. Good looking decor depends on the balloons being sized precisely.

Follow this guide and you will get better results from your balloons.

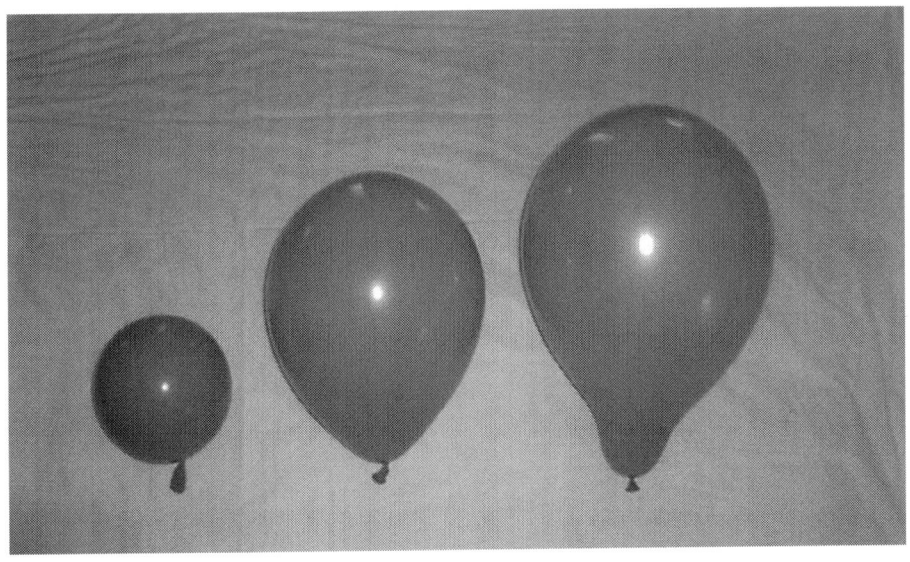

Perfectly round- underinflated, teardrop- just right, light bulb- going to pop

How To Make a Balloon Water Weight

Water weights are very convenient weights. They really help in a pinch, because if you're setting up at an event and you realize that you don't have enough weights with you, ie the client adds more decor on the spot, well you probably have some extra balloons.

First of all, it's really important to double stuff the balloon! I can't stress this enough! By double stuffing the balloon, you ensure that even if there is a little pinhole in the balloon, the water will not leak out.

To double stuff, take two 11" balloons- colors don't necessarily matter, but if you won't be wrapping the balloons in paper, make sure it coordinates with the rest of the decor. Choose which balloon will be the inside balloon. Fold the balloon lengthwise in quarters. This will make a nice little point that will make it easier to stuff one balloon inside the other. Thread the quartered balloon into the other balloon, making sure that the nozzles of the balloons are stacked one on top of the other.

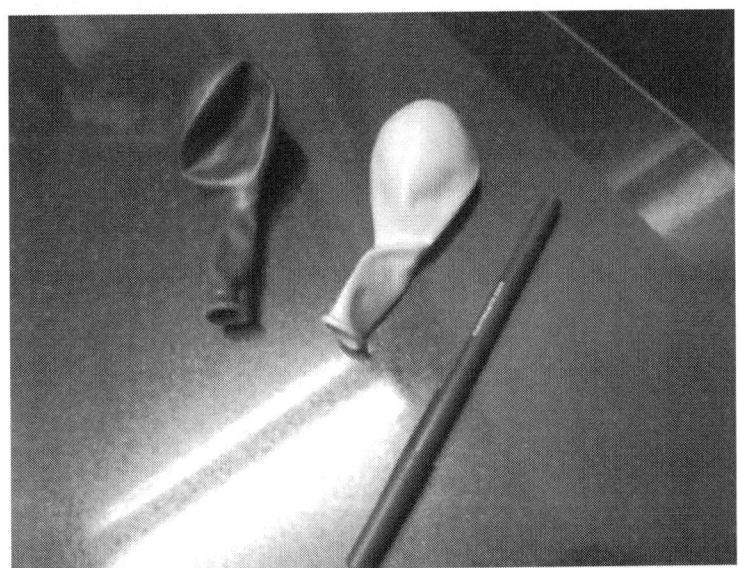

Now, just like making regular water balloons, stretch BOTH nozzles over the water spigot in the sink. Make sure that you are using both nozzles as one, or you will have a big mess. Now fill the bowl of the balloon until it just stretches a little bit- about the size of a baseball (maximum). Do NOT fill the balloon all the way. You just want enough weight to hold down a bouquet, but you want the balloon to stay squishy and strong.

Tie both balloons as if they are one. Some will say that you only need to tie the inner balloon, but I've always found it works better to tie both of them together.

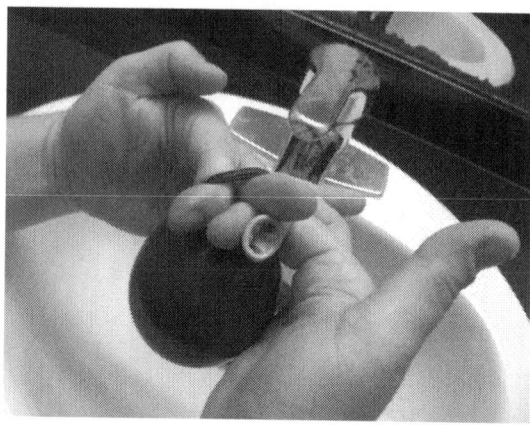

Now, you have a water weight. You can stop here, and tie the balloon bouquet to it as is, or you can wrap it with paper to make it look more decorative.

Assuming you want to wrap it, you first need to make an attachment point. Take a piece of ribbon, find the center, and tie it around the neck of the balloons. Make a double knot, and set aside.

Take 2-3 sheets of mylar paper, cello paper, tissue paper, or even plastic tablecloth-or any combination thereof. Figure out which color you want to be the base of the weight, and put that one on the bottom. Lay the next piece of paper on top of the first, slightly offset so that it makes a sort of star. Take the 3rd piece and do the same.

If you just drop the water weight in the middle of the papers and wrap it that way, it will look nice, but it will wobble from side to side. This could be a good thing if you want that effect, but if you don't, you need to create a flat surface. To make a flat surface, take something flat and put it on top of the paper. An easy flat object to put on the paper as a base is money- a quarter is a good size, but a nickel will work as well. It's handy and most people have it in their purse or pocket.

After you put the coin on the bottom, drop the weight on top of it. Take the ribbons that you have tied to the balloon in one hand, and with the other, reach under the papers and grab them and bring the corners together- making a little bundle with the weight in the middle. Be careful to make sure that you don't trap the ribbon inside the wrapped weight. Grab the whole thing around the neck, and tie a piece of ribbon around it to secure it. The tighter you tie the ribbon, the nicer it will look.

After you tie your helium balloons to the weight you can fluff out the pieces of paper to make it look nice and decorative.

There you have your water weight!

If these instructions seemed difficult to follow, here is a link to a video that will show you how to wrap the weight http://youtu.be/I5CVCB6cyBI

How To Make a Balloon Bouquet

To start, I recommend finding the video I made on the same subject (http://youtu.be/aACX7hOTucU), it's easier to follow with the visual. Having said that, here's how you arrange a balloon bouquet:

To begin, we'll use only 5 balloons. You can always add more later once you learn the technique, but this is a good number to start with. Generally speaking, you always want odd numbers, so the center will be something to look at and not the negative space between the balloons. It's also important to note that these instructions are for latex balloons only. Due to the California Balloon Laws, you don't want to use this method with mylar balloons.

Have the balloons on long ribbons, it will make everything else much easier.

Put all five balloons in your hand, coming out the top, all the balloons should be grouped together in one big "lollipop" formation, floating just above your hand.

Hold your hand at about waist height. Take the first balloon and bring it up as high as you can without hitting the ceiling or losing the string.

Take the second balloon, and without releasing all of the balloons, loosen your hand just enough to enable you to move the balloon. Pull it up until the top of the second balloon just touches the bottom of the first balloon. We call this method making them "kiss".

Continue through the rest of the balloons, making each balloon just kiss the balloon above it.

If you are starting to get short ribbons from the top balloons, tie them to the other balloons that you've already arranged and continue.

Once you have all five balloons arranged, tie a knot connecting all of the ribbons together. The knot should be a few inches below the bottom balloon.

To set the final height of the arrangement, use your body templates. That means measure the length of the ribbon under the last balloon against parts of your body. I usually measure from the hand that is holding the balloon straight across my outstretched arm to the shoulder of the same arm. That's the first height. The next height would be from my hand, across my outstretched arm to the center of my chest, then to the other shoulder, then across my full wingspan.

Once you've set your height, tie a knot where you want to connect to the anchor. Use this knot as a guide for tying onto your weight. This is the way that you can make beautiful consistent arrangements throughout the entire room.

How to Curl Ribbon

I want to share with you how to curl a ribbon. Now I know what you're thinking, you're thinking, "Hey, that's so obvious. Of course all I do is I just take my scissors, open them up and get going." Well, not quite. Actually, the fact of the matter is that you don't need to open your scissors. If you're using sharp scissors, it's even kind of dangerous because it's not the blade that curls the ribbon, it's actually just the pressure against the flat edge so you can keep your scissors closed and safe and still curl your ribbon.

What you're going to do is you're going to take your scissors, closed scissors, and I always make sure that I have a blunt tip because it really can be detrimental if you've got one of those pointy ones and you accidentally go up just a little bit too far. What you're going to do is you're going to take your straight edge here, you're going to look at the natural curl of the ribbon and you're going to go on the back side. I use this kind of holographic ribbon so I know that the flat side or the not shining side is the side that I'm going to curl. If you're using more of a regular curling ribbon, if you follow the curl and you go on the underside of the curl, then you're going to get a nice result.

So what you're going to do is you're going to just take your flat edge, take your thumb and put a nice even pressure, not too tight, not too loose, and kind of scrape the ribbon across your edge like that, and you're going to get a nice curl. If you want a tighter curl, put more pressure and if you want a looser your curl, back off the pressure a little. And there you go, that's how to curl a ribbon. If you prefer to watch a video, here's a link: http://youtu.be/uwP-DQEFLHzI

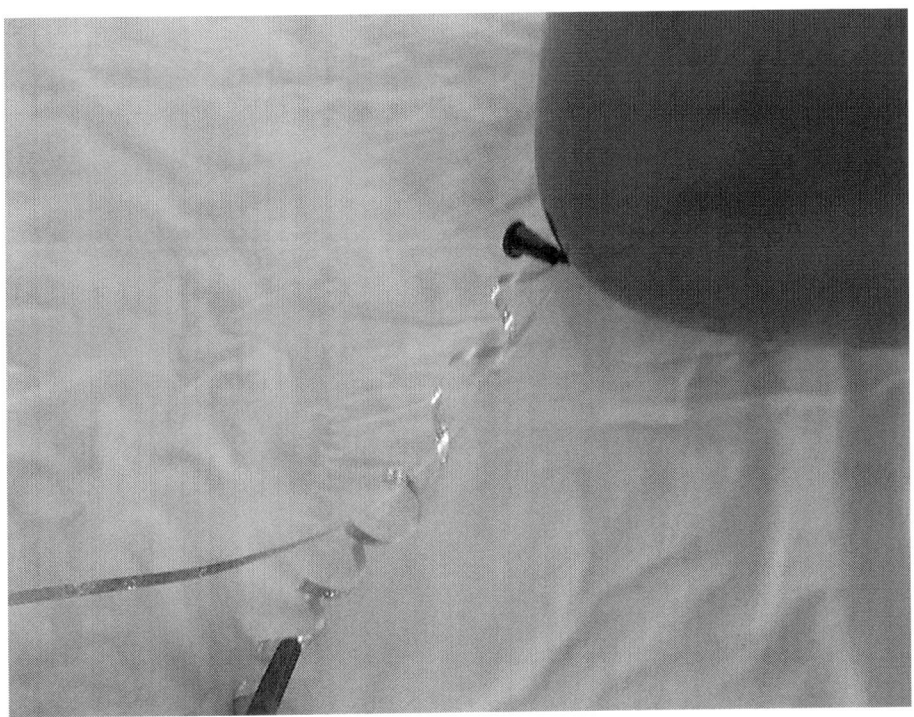

How To Get a Balloon Off Of The Ceiling

Has it ever happened that you were using helium balloons for an event and one of the balloons escaped to the ceiling? It doesn't sound like that big of a deal, it will come down eventually, right? True, if it's an 11" balloon, it will come down in around 24 hours or so. If it's a mylar balloon, it might be a couple of weeks, or even months.

Some venues will charge you $100 or more for every lost balloon! So, what's a person to do? Bring a really long pole with a pair of scissors awkwardly taped to it? Try dangerous methods like bibi guns or something like that?

The answer is much simpler- go fishing! It's really quite simple, take another helium balloon, inflated a little larger than the one you lost, and put a loop of duck tape on the top of the balloon. Have the balloon tied to a really long ribbon, or better yet, keep the ribbon attached to the spool so you can lengthen and shorten as needed.

Let the balloon go up to the ceiling and gently tap the wayward balloon. The balloon should stick to the duck tape. Once you've made the connection, gently reel it back in. It's that easy.

Here's a link to a video for those who are more visual: http://youtu.be/AgMjq1EMBnM

How Long Will a Balloon Float and Can You Make It Float Longer?

The average float time for an 11" latex balloon is about 18 hours. Some 12" balloons that are sold at party stores will only float for about 12 hours. Because balloons are very porous, and the helium molecule is really small, the helium seeps through the walls of the balloon.

The good news is that you can extend the float time of the balloon with a product called Hi-Float. Hi-float is a water-based gel that you put inside the balloon to seal the pores of the balloon, so that it will retain the helium longer. Hi-floated balloons can even last up to a few weeks!

To use hi-float, pre-inflate all the balloons- that is fill them up with air, and then let all the air back out. This is to identify problems, such as pin-holes and windows, that will cause the balloon to pop upon inflation. You want to weed out the bad balloons before you put the hi-float in because it make a big gooey mess if the balloon pops afterwards!

After you've pre-inflated your balloon, squirt the recommended amount of hi-float into the balloon, (measurements provided w/ product), then squish it around so that it coats the entire bowl of the balloon. Be careful to keep it out of the neck of the balloon or you'll have a hard time tying it.

Inflate and tie your balloon. If the balloon sinks, it's probably because you've used too much hi-float. If it wobbles from side-to-side, it will probably float just fine once the hi-float dries.

This is a great option for deliveries or multi- day events. Something that's important to note, Hi-float doesn't do very well outside with weather and really works better indoors.

How to Make a Balloon Arch/ Column

This is a hard one to do in writing, but I'll try :-) If you find it hard to follow, look for the video version (http://youtu.be/hQL5lJegmHc), and that should help.

First of all, when you're making a "spiral" arch, it is really really important that all of the balloons are properly sized. Incorrectly sized balloons can really ruin the look of the arch. The actual balloon size is relative to the size of balloons you are using and the size of the arch, but it's critical that all the balloons in the arch are the same size (Until you get into advanced shaping techniques, but that's another topic).

Unless your arch is framed, you're probably using helium. The easiest way to wrap the balloons onto the fishing line, or dacron arch line, is by stretching the line between two chairs. Then you can wrap the balloons onto the taught line. Make sure that it's well secured, but with a little bit of slack. As it grows, the lift will fight against you a bit.

Most "spiral" arches are created using a four- pack of balloons. You make that by creating two duplets of balloons, (two balloons tied together by their necks), and twisting them together.

So, take the four balloons, and arrange them in the color pattern that you are trying to create. Make sure to continue the same order throughout the arch.

Wedge the string between two of the balloon in the quad. Either wrap the balloons with the string to secure, or rotate the two balloons that are straddling the string around each other.

Take the next quad, line it up in the right place and repeat the procedure.

Keep repeating the same steps, consistently rotating either to the right or to the left. You will notice that there is a sweet spot where the balloons are just offset and seem to nestle in. Also, it's best if you try not to drag the balloons across the line as that may result in friction tears. After about four clusters you will see the pattern emerging.

To finish it off, tie each side to an anchor. There will be a lot of lift, so be sure that they are heavy enough! An easy to find anchor is a 2.5 gallon water bottle, just tie on to the handle, wrap it with some pretty paper, and you're ready to go.

To make a column the steps are the same, but you would use a baseplate and a pole, and the balloons would be air-filled instead of helium filled.

Twist together 4 balloons and attach to pole or fishing line

Stack up more quads, one on top of the other

And keep adding more quads, until you have the length of arch you want, or the pole is covered.

And then you will have beautiful columns

How Are Balloons Affected By Temperature?

Has it ever happened to you that you had your balloons set up in the morning for an outdoor event, and around noon all the balloons started popping? Or perhaps your balloons were inflated before the venue turned on the air conditioning, and by the time your party started, all the mylars looked like they had lost half of their volume?

Why is this? Most people take their balloons for granted as a decor medium, and rarely think about the science behind their decorations. Floating balloons are filled with a gas called helium. Helium is an inert gas that is lighter than air, (which is why it makes the balloons float). Though helium is not flammable or explosive, it is a gas and therefore reacts quickly to changes in temperature.

If the temperature is higher than it was at inflation, the gas will expand, which can cause the balloon to pop. If the temperature is lower than it was at the time of inflation, the gas will contract and the balloon will look as though it's not full. There's still enough helium to provide the necessary lift to the balloon, so that it will float, but it may look as though it's only half- full.

So, now that you know this, what can you do to prevent temperature related balloon disasters? Well, there are a couple of things that can be done:

1. If you expect that the event will be in an air-conditioned room, try to inflate the balloons under the same conditions.

2. If you think that the event will be hotter than the room where you're inflating the balloons, or if you're worried that it will get hotter throughout the day, (a condition that we often have to worry about with balloons in San Diego), then slightly under-inflate your balloons to account for the gas expansion as the temperature rises.

Paying attention to the atmospheric conditions of the room in which you are doing your inflation, and anticipating the temperature of the event will greatly reduce temperature related balloon malfunctions.

One more thing to note, balloons go through a natural oxidization process, so over time inflated balloons can take on a velvety texture. This process goes much faster outdoors or in smoky environments. It's rarely an issue, but now you know the answer to the trivia question: Why do the balloons look less shiny over time? ☺

Formula to Fill a Ceiling with Balloons

If you are trying to fill a ceiling with balloon, it can be very frustrating to try to figure out exactly how many balloons and how much helium you actually need.

But, fear not, there is a formula to help you. Now, please bear in mind that this formula is specifically for 11" balloons. Are you ready, ok- here it is:

(L X W) / 0.66

That's length x width divided by 0.66.

So, let's pretend that we have a space that's 10 x 10 (your average trade show booth size). According to our formula, L x W would be 10 x 10 = 100.

100/ 0.66 = 152 (well, really 151 and some change, but it's difficult to cut a balloon in half, so we'll round up).

So, we'd need 152 balloons.

If you were to do this for a dance floor, most dance floors are some combination of 18 x 18 - 24 x 24. For best results check with your venue to find out the actual size of your dancefloor.

Again, just to save you from scrolling up to the top to see the formula, it is: (L x W) / 0.66

Someone who has a better understanding of geometry

might be able to tell you how that formula works, I don't know all the math involved to get there, I just know that when I'm doing events, I've found the formula to be a reliable guideline.

Just to remind you, this formula only works for 11" balloons. If you are using 16" balloons or 3' balloons, it would be a different formula (for a different article). Don't use 9" balloons or smaller as they won't float very long at all.

Anyway, now you know how to save yourself from getting either too many or too few balloons.

A couple of other useful tips:

An 11" balloon has an average float time of 18 hours.

A tank of helium that has 110 cubic feet of helium can inflate approximately 200 11" balloons.*

A tank of helium that has 220 cubic feet of helium can inflate approximately 400 11" balloons. *

(*It's actually a little bit more, but I always prefer to underestimate a little rather than overestimate, so I never find myself short of materials on the job site.)

The best balloons to use are either Qualatex or Betallic. I would stay away from some of the cheaper brands of balloons as the float time is dramatically decreased. Also, the cheaper balloons pop more, so you're not really saving much.

Testimonials

From Google Reviews:

ASPS, Inc. - a month ago

Sandi and her staff were amazing. They provided the balloons for our booth at a recent convention in San Diego. The balloons looked as fresh on day 4 as they did on day 1. Everyone who visited our booth during the convention commented on how our booth looked the best. We will definitely use Balloon Utopia again for any of our conventions in San Diego

Mar 17, 2011 by smmerlo2002

I attended a large event at the Westin on West Broadway in San Francisco, and the balloons, which were created by Balloon Utopia, were fabulous! They created a huge wall of balloons containing the company's logo, as well as displays throughout the conference room and the lobby. It's amazing how much the balloons contribute to the spirit of the event. They did a fabulous job! I highly recommend Balloon Utopia for an upbeat and fun corporate event.

From Yelp :

Mark R. Placentia, Ca 5/10/2011

The 8' tall balloon man stopped everyone in front of our booth!

Kristine G. San Diego, CA

3/7/2011 Balloon Utopia was great! I couldn't believe what Sandi could do with balloons! It's amazing! From lighted palm trees to just the right colors. They were flexible and helpful! They even helped us with our own dilema of how to hang up signs so they were visible...using balloons! Great Job, Thanks for working with us and helping make our event look great!

Transcriptions from video testimonials:

Beth Licha, Soille San Diego Hebrew Day School

Hi, I'm Beth Licha, the director of admissions for Soille San Diego Hebrew Day School. We hired Balloon Utopia to be with us at a community booth at the Yom Ha'atzma'ut festival. It's a very large festival with lots of vendors and lots of organizations representing. And I have to say that I can't imagine doing it without Balloon Utopia. They were fantastic! Our objective was to meet new families and to have an opportunity to tell them about our school. And if we didn't have Balloon Utopia there, entertaining the children and creating a line, because EVERYONE wanted a balloon, I wouldn't have had the opportunity to talk with all of their parents. They would have walked by quicker than a heartbeat. There were other schools there and none of them had lines. I can't imagine how they met anyone because people aren't coming to the fair to talk about school. But I met tons of people and got lots of family information, contacts that I could follow up with afterwards. Because those parents were a captive audience while they waited for their children.

Eric Kurit- Upside Down Iceberg

Hey, this is Eric Kurit from Upside Down Iceberg, and I want to give a quick shout out to Balloon Utopia who did all the balloons for this event. You can tell what a huge difference these balloons are making . And if you want to make a big bang at your event (well, you'd pop them, so don't do that), but if you want to make a big stand out and make a huge difference you can tell how awesome they are, they really make a huge thing- when you've got something that's standing out it makes a big difference.

You know, really something different. You know, normally people put up a sign, what's that, a sign, that doesn't do anything, you want something big. That's what you really want to do- Balloon Utopia

Maria – Mk Pure Diamond Events

Hi I'm Maria with MK Pure Diamond events and today we used a new marketing system that I am so excited about. We had a booth at the bridal bazaar and our brides got to text in their email and name for a drawing. And I am so excited, I can't wait to see who the winner is. We used a wonderful product and I highly recommend it.

Wendi – Skyline (tradeshow booth builders)

Hi, my name is Wendi and I'm with Skyline. My client is Vertafore, and when they first contacted me asking about putting some balloons on the booth, I was a little skeptical, but as soon as I walked up on the show floor today- it looked incredible! The colors and the way that they customized it by putting up the "20"s- it just looks great and I couldn't be happier.

Nancy- Vertafore

Hi, I'm Nancy with Vertafore, and we're a Washington based company. We were looking for something exciting to do with the 20 year anniversary of one of our products and we called Balloon Utopia for some advice. And all I wanted was some balloons that I could put around my posts. Sandi created this wonderful masterpiece, with arches, which at first I was skeptical about. But it was fabulous when I got here. Unbelieveable. Yellow, orange- that's all I told her. It looks great, we love it, good job.

Carolyn Navarra President of the Navarra Group

Hi. I'm Carolyn Navarra, President of The Navarra Group. In partnership with ABC Channel 10 here in San Diego we are putting on this school expo. We needed balloons so we called Balloon Utopia and they are just what their name is all about. It's the perfect place to get something that would be an addition to an event to make it more festive and so that people are aware there is a special occasion going on.

And they are special; Sandi was able to come in and improvise something that we didn't even realize we were could order on the last minute and day of the event. She did an amazing job; their service, their pricing structure and the actual presentation is Utopia.

So if you're looking for a great place to spruce up any event or any occasion – expos, bar mitzvahs, parties or whatever you might need – call Balloon Utopia because they're an amazing place to do business with."

Mike Koenigs from Traffic Geyser and Instant Customer

This is Mike Koenigs from Traffic Geyser and Instant Customer. I wanted to put together a heartfelt thank you and a little testimonial for Sandi from Balloon Utopia. Sandi has been doing all of our sets and stage work for all of our events; putting together remarkable, remarkable stage sets and interestingly enough, doing it with balloons.

Sandi is unbelievably creative. The last time we had our Main Street Marketing Machines launch and then right after that, we had something called Make Market Launch. What's so cool is she put together great signs; great props. All of the balloons just looked magnificent. Every single one of our events ends up being recorded, videotaped and then made available as a product to all of our customers. For something like that, we really, really need something that has a super high degree of value.

Sandi is just talented and easy to work with. Our event coordinator, Event Manager Jessie Schwartzburg, talks about how remarkable Balloon Utopia is and how easy they are to work with. She's also never missed a deadline.

What I can tell you is, if you are looking for some way of creating a truly remarkable experience for an event to promote your brand and company in any type of a situation, you've got to talk to Sandi. If you want to work with someone who is consistently delivering a great product – something that's really creative – contact Sandi. Working with Sandi at Balloon Utopia is just hands-free; you don't have to think about doing a lot of coordinating. She just knows what to do and in my opinion and from my experience, she's hit a homerun, every single time.

So take it from me, Mike Koenigs from Traffic Geyser and Instant Customer, Sandi is the kind of person that you want to work with. Check out Balloon Utopia and look at some of the pictures, look at some of the stage work she's done and look at her balloon creations; they are remarkable and unique. When you work with Sandi and Balloon Utopia, you're creating an experience that clients and customers will like and talk about for a long time.

30' Stage Wall
Photo By Debbie LeFever
Look For Volume 2 of the Ultimate Guide To Inflating Profits to Learn More About Banquets, Meetings & Stages

Bonus Section :
Using Balloons For Grand Openings

Grand Opening Décor

Congratulations! After months, maybe even years of planning, the building is built, the fixtures in place and you're ready to plan your official Grand Opening event! So many little details to think about. First of all, how do you let people know about your grand opening? We'll leave most of the various advertising and marketing ideas for another article and talk about the eye catching decorations. Why use grand opening balloon décor? Balloons generate excitement, and carry with them the message of fun and happiness. By touching the subconscious heartstrings of your potential customers, you are getting an instant warm fuzzy. Also, balloons are highly visible, totally customizable and a great cost effective way to get more coverage for your money.

There are 3 types of grand opening balloon décor:

- Attention getting décor to be seen from far away
- Attention getting décor to be seen from parking lot to bring people into store
- Ambient décor inside store to generate excitement and drive impulse buys

Let's start by discussing outdoor décor for a minute. The key to outdoor décor is to plan with weather conditions in mind. Don't use dark colors, like black, blue, green or purple as they absorb heat and could pop on hot days. Do anchor your balloons to something that fixed in the ground whenever possible, for example, a sign post, or a light. Remember that balloons are susceptible to wind, even as little as 4 miles an hour, so plan décor that is well anchored and designed to work with the wind. I don't recommend using bouquets of balloons outdoors, as they tend to tangle, but instead would go for topiary kites or clusters of balloons where there is a single anchor point. Look to wide ribbons to add that extra rhythm and movement. For columns and arches, make sure that you have a strong internal framework and a solid base with a large footprint. The taller your décor, the bigger the footprint needs to be. We usually use 150 lb steel baseplates that have a 2' footprint for our outdoor columns and arches. Even with that, we sometimes need to add weight to stabilize against the wind. One last thing that's important to note for outdoor décor, even if you're not in California, it's a good idea to follow the California balloon laws. That is that every mylar balloon must be individually weighted, and no balloons can be attatched to an electrically conducive material. Following these guidelines makes for a better environmental impact, and reduces the risk of an inadvertent power failure. Note that latex balloons are completely biodegradeable, but none-the-less should be properly handled.

Now, let's return to our 3 types of grand opening décor. The first, décor that can be seen from far away is designed to let people know from beyond the parking lot (maybe even the freeway or main road) that something special is happening in this area. Remember that the higher you go, the smaller things appear, so plan accordingly. More is better. Sure, one streamer will show people where you are, but 5 of them will make them really wonder what is going on. So, as you plan your décor, ask yourself if your purpose is to mark the area for people who already know they are coming to you- that is as a directional, or are you trying to get people to pull over and come to you when they weren't yet aware that they wanted to? If you are only trying to mark the entrance for people already in the know, one floating column or streamer may well be enough. If, on the other hand, you want to draw a crowd from all over, then multiple pieces are better. The top three sellers for attraction décor are Floating columns, floating mini columns and streamers. The difference between them is the look, and girth of the design. All can be effective.

The second type of décor, that is the entrance decor, is designed to build interest and let people already in the parking lot, or general vicinity, know that something special is happening here. The décor can be as simple as a couple of columns, or an arch, or as elaborate as a faux entrance façade that creates a scene and entices people to use it as a photo backdrop as well. The main difference is that while the simple décor marks the spot, the more elaborate style becomes a talking point and a branding item. (The pictures will be shared with others of course, so make sure that the store logo is incorporated in some way).   I've seen events where people were so excited about the entrance that they called friends from all over to come and see it. These people then went into the store, of course, to see what all the excitement is about.

While there are as many different design options as there are types of stores, I want to address some of the most common; 1) the spiral arch- a high visual energy piece, that while very effective in some cases, is often overused by default. I personally prefer the look of 2 columns with a string of pearls arch, or even double pearls. We'll talk more about a perfect use for the spiral arch once we get to the interior décor.   2) the columns- there are many different styles of columns, from your standard spiral to people sculptures. If you're going to use standard spiral columns, make the most of the visual energy they produce by building them so that they spiral into each other. This way the eye is led right into the store. There are other types of columns as well, some of them are better than others if you want to use it as a branding item. Linear columns, which have more of a "Flat" look, and are built on a grid system, give an excellent surface to superimpose signs or logos. Sculpture style columns, like the clowns or carrots, are a fun way to give a clue as to what's inside the store. Both of these make for excellent photo backdrops as well. For evening events putting lights inside of your balloons and turning them into lamps is very effective. This special effect is both attention getting, beautiful and conversation starting. 3) Linear Arch- like the linear columns, an arch based on a grid system is perfect for inserting logos or signage. Also, it's a different look, so may draw more curious bystanders. 4) Topiary sculpture entrance tunnel- this is by far the most elaborate. Using a topiary sculpture design system, ANY shape, logo, mascot or concept can be brought to life—larger than life. This is by far the more expensive option, but depending on your event and target demographic, may give the best ROI. This is giant walk-through piece of art. It's not just an entrance, it's an experience.

Now let's move inside. Here is a perfect place for those spiral arches. The spiral arch leads the eye up one side, and down the other. So if there are two aisles that you want people to browse, it's a great way to highlight both. Other types of décor designed to direct the eye to products of interest range from the simple, but effective bouquet of balloons, to the more elaborate hanging sculptures. Obviously, in order to retain as much real estate as possible for products and customers, making good use of your vertical space is going to be key. Decorate the air and the whole room will come alive. Bouquets or small sculptures on end caps make for great attention getting décor, thereby increasing those impulse buys. There is a product called hi-float that can be added to the inside of the balloon before it is inflated that will dramatically increase it's float time. With this product, you can keep that grand opening excitement alive for the whole week!

Fun Topiary Balls Attract Attention From Afar

Linear Columns supporting sign

Carrot columns

Cloud 9's

Ballerina Sculpture

Linear Column and floating mini columns

Standard spiral columns and linear arch

Topiary Design Logo Scene

Hi Flying Streamer

Pencil Columns and jumping string of pearl arches

Mini bouquets at cash registers

Standard columns w/ string of pearls arch

Long lasting Mylar Balloon Columns w/ spirals pointing into each other

10' Walk-through baseball

Bouquets marking promos

Juggling Clowns

Wild Columns Make Everyone Wonder What Is Going On Inside The Store

RESOURCES

- There are a ton of photos on the Balloon Utopia website, which can be found at http://www.balloonutopia.com . In the various galleries are many more examples of the types of décor discussed above.

- To see some more "How To" videos, check out my YouTube Channel: http://www.youtube.com/sandiballoon

- I also have some step-by-step photo tutorials at http://snapguide.com/sandi-masori/

- Here is my resource page where you can learn more about various marketing programs and other online resources that I use: http://www.sandirecommends.com

- Here is my internet marketing coaching site: Http://www.webcoach4you.com

ABOUT THE AUTHOR

Sandi Masori has been a balloon industry leader and educator since 1994. In 2010, Wanting to make her own business website get better results, Sandi started studying marketing, search engine optimization, social media and cross- channel marketing. After a few years of trying to juggle both identities, Sandi realized that she could combine both passions into one and serve her corporate clients best by using balloons as a marketing tool, along side the other tools in her marketing bag of tricks. Sandi currently lives in San Diego, Ca with her husband and children, where she runs Balloon Utopia and the Masori Group.

NOTES

The Ultimate Guide to Inflating Your Trade Show Profits

Manufactured by Amazon.ca
Bolton, ON